PRISCILLA'S ANGELS

George and Linda B

PRISCILLA'S ANGELS

Priscilla is six years old when she lost her parents and younger brother to the Spanish flu epidemic in 1918. She moved in with her Aunt Dora. With much effort, Priscilla has become a welcome member of the new family, but trouble is on the way, and her guardian angels are working overtime to keep her safe. All her friends in the yard of the large Victorian house are helping to keep the adults from ruining her life as well as their own. It won't be long before the action gets out of hand and Cilla and others will be falling from the sky.

Priscilla is now feeling more comfortable in her beautiful new home. Her Aunt Dora is even including her in the plans for the upcoming wedding. As she is feeling closer to Dora, she is sensing a greater bond with her grandfather as well; however, the same is not true of Smithfield, Dora's fiancé.

Cilla feels the groom is jealous of her blossoming relationship with his future bride and his soon-to-be father-in-law. Cilla has moved him from center stage, and this results in the young orphan's increased uneasiness. What can she do? First, she talked to her yard friends and most importantly asked God for help.

Cilla wandered through her domain and visited several friends. She told them of the wedding in the next few weeks to be held in the yard. After the ceremony, Professor Smyth's home will be a gift to the newlyweds. At present, Priscilla will be living with the married pair, and Aunt Dora's new husband is obviously uncomfortable with the prospect.

Priscilla once lived on a farm far into the countryside; however, because of the Spanish flu epidemic and the death of her mother, father, and younger brother, Cilla is now being cared for by her Aunt Dora. At first, Priscilla was an unwelcome complication to her aunt and grandfather's lives.

However, several months ago, yellowjackets threatened to stop Dora from holding an outdoor celebration with her sorority sisters; Cilla endeared herself to them when she orchestrated a miracle by using her yard friends and saved the day by ridding her grandad's property of these unwanted and dangerous insects.

Priscilla is now a fully honored and valued member of Aunt Dora's and Professor Smyth's family. Both Dora and Grandfather Smyth now recognize Cilla's special capabilities and "imaginary friends," who they originally dismissed. She sees her playmates daily and spends hours reading to them selections from the books in her grandfather's massive library.

Today Cilla listened to a new friend whom she had taught to read. This new friend, Martha, is the wife of the tiny white-haired man, Sid, who runs the Bird Rider's flight school. When the reading session was over, Priscilla asked those listening for ideas on how to deal with Smithfield. Wanda, the commander of the nymph army, suggested she approach the problem like a military campaign. "You out-maneuver Dora's fiancé and blindside him by hitting him at his weakest point." Cilla wondered what all those words meant; she had no idea what Wanda just said.

Priscilla asked, "Wanda, could you explain what you just said?"

Wanda spoke with authority, "When Smithfield comes to visit Dora and your grandfather, ask him if he will do you a big favor, and then bring him to the yard. We will be waiting for him and put on a show that he will either run like a coward from or understand you are someone to respect and honor."

Priscilla said, "I appreciate your concern and willingness to do this for me, but I am not sure it would result in an improvement in our relationship."

Wanda then shouted, "Let Sid, the Bird Rider, shrink him down to our size, and we will carry him down to the pond and feed him to the bullfrogs!"

Cilla was shocked but replied, "The bullfrog thing is over the top, but the part about shrinking him down to experience what it is like to see life from a different level could work."

Smithfield Goodfellow had always succeeded; he always got his way. His law practice was highly successful, and now he was to marry the most beautiful, highly educated, and most desired woman in the city. Her father (Professor Smyth) was the dean of the law school from which he graduated, of course, at the top of his class. His concern was the sudden appearance of Dora's niece, Priscilla. He knew he had to be careful not to antagonize the six-year-old orphan whom he disliked greatly, all the while Cilla did represent an opportunity to take control of the entire Smyth family's estate and financial holdings.

With his marriage to Dora, his new bride's half of the Smyth's estate would be under his control, and if he could control Cilla's inheritance and assets, he would have it all. He asked the professor, without Dora's knowledge, about Cilla's financial status.

Cilla's grandfather assured Smithfield that the young child would never lack for anything because of the sale of her family's farm, and unknown to Priscilla and Dora, Cilla's paternal grandfather just died and left her, as his only heir, a fortune ten times that of Professor Smyth's own estate. And, of course, Cilla inherits half of his (Professor Smyth's) substantial estate as well.

The cunning lawyer, though now trying to endear himself to the professor, was always jealous and resentful of his old law teacher. Smithfield could not wait to collect the man's entire estate including his daughter's and now potentially his soon-to-be step-niece.

Smithfield Goodfellow was counting on Priscilla's fascination and obsession over her imaginary world. He knew he could use it against her. As Dora's husband, he could very likely prove Cilla was unable to conduct her own affairs, and he, of course, would be declared her guardian. From that point forward, he could control Dora's, Professor Smyth's, and Priscilla's wealth as his own.

Cilla sensed an undeclared war between Smithfield and herself.

When alone with her aunt, Priscilla asked Dora if she was truly in love with Smithfield and if she was sure of her decision to marry him. Aunt Dora meekly answered, "Well, Smithfield is an excellent catch. My father and he have much in common, and your grand-father has graciously promised to deed us this house and property, to include his prized library once we are together. It is time I am married, and I feel I may find none better." Cilla now knew she must act.

The intuitive orphan did not know how she knew, but she knew Smithfield was evil. It was time to put a plan together to expose his motives and discover if he really cared for Dora and her family.

Cilla consulted Sir Boss, the regal squirrel that ruled over the entire yard where she lived. He reined from the large oak tree on the back property line. To go there, she had to have Sid shrink her to a size enabling her to fly on the back of a bird mount to the top of the oak. When she arrived, Sir Boss welcomed her like a royal guest. He was most appreciative of her removing from his domain the dangerous invading yellowjackets several months ago.

Sir Boss told Cilla that his resources and warriors were at her complete disposal. Because of her past honorable assistance, her wish was his command. Priscilla thanked him for his offer and accepted. She told Sir Boss that she would need not only the nymph bee riders but also others not usually involved in a complex operation.

For Cilla's plan to work, she needed the most frightening animal in the entire yard kingdom. She therefore sought out the top predator in her world. His name was Malcom Hawk. He often sat at the top of the roof from which he kept a watch on the entire yard and beyond. Through an agreement with Sir Boss, Malcom only hunted beyond the yard. Otherwise, he was like a sentinel that kept watch for everyone's protection. Nothing escaped his keen eyesight and speed of flight. From his perch, he could reach anywhere in the yard in seconds.

Priscilla's plan was to entice Smithfield to go on a grand adventure he could not turn down. Once committed, he would have to play by her rules and not by the rules he normally used to win. Cilla knew Smithfield was to visit their home for a formal but private dinner party with Dora, Professor Smyth, and herself. During this time, she would offer him an opportunity to visit her imaginary world. She thought he would have to accept or seem dismissive to her childlike and innocent offer.

The long-anticipated evening came, and Smithfield arrived promptly at the front door. Professor Smyth welcomed his future son-in-law warmly and took him to his library for a drink and conversation. Dora and she were busy setting the dining room table with all the required silverware, napkins, and glasses. Cilla asked Dora, "Would you and grandfather mind if I asked Smithfield to walk alone with me in the yard after we have finished our dinner and before I go to bed?"

Dora didn't quite understand but said, "If it is important to you, by all means you may ask him to go, but don't be disappointed if he refuses."

As the four of them were finishing dinner, Cilla asked Smithfield if he would do her a special favor. He was initially taken by surprise but thought it would not look good for him to refuse.

Priscilla, in a very innocent voice, asked, "Good Sir, I have something I would like to show you in the yard. It is only for you alone. Would you do me the honor of accompanying me there?"

Professor Smyth immediately apologized for his impertinent granddaughter, "Smithfield, you are under no obligation to grant Cilla her request!"

Smithfield responded, with an inquisitive tone in his voice, "Well, well, how could I refuse such an interesting offer?"

Cilla had set the hook. She got up from her chair and went to Smithfield, took his hand in hers, and led him out into the yard. Professor Smyth and Dora looked on with curiosity but held their comments.

As they left the house, Cilla directed Smithfield's attention to the yard, "Sir, the old hickory stump over there is slowly rotting but holds an interesting treasure seldom seen. Would you like to see it?"

Smithfield, trying to get this little excursion over quickly, replied, "Yes, of course, I would like to see your treasure."

He thought, *This is a great opportunity; the more I witness her inability to distinguish reality from fantasy, the more evidence I will have to take control of her fortune.*

The evening light was beginning to fade, and the stump was in the darkest part of the yard. The young conspirator directed Smithfield, "Look within the stump; if it is dark enough, you will see a pale green light. This is foxfire. It is a fungus that can grow within rotting wood and glows. It is rarely seen, and I wanted to share it with you." Cilla had taken Smithfield to the Bird Rider's headquarters. Once there, Sid waved his hand and shrunk Smithfield and Cilla to one, one-hundredth of their normal size.

Within seconds, Malcom swooped down and seized Priscilla and Smithfield in his mighty talons. Cilla screeched as loud as she could. The sound was ear-splitting, and Smithfield almost fainted from shock. The mighty hawk flew above the pond and dropped them toward the center of the now enormous-looking body of water. It was like a huge lake to the two shrunk humans.

As they hit the water, the air was forced out of their lungs. Smithfield resurfaced first and was coughing out water. Priscilla soon resurfaced and acted as if she could not swim and was about to drown. Smithfield, instead of assisting Cilla, swam for a floating log. He failed the test.

A dragonfly swooped down and plucked Priscilla out of the water and headed toward the shore.

Wanda, the bee rider nymph warrior commander, met Cilla on the shore. She confirmed with Priscilla that Smithfield failed his test. She then signaled her assistants for the next step to begin. The muskrat allowed Cilla to hop on his back, and they swam out to the log where Smithfield was stranded.

Cilla on arrival asked him, "Do you understand where you are?"

He was very stunned and whispered, "We are inside your imaginary world?"

Priscilla smiled and said, "Yes, I am surprised you recognize your situation, and by the way, I wouldn't swim from this log; there are very hungry bullfrogs around here, and you are just the right size to be a wonderfully filling meal for one of them."

Smithfield, extremely stunned, squeaks, "What do you want, and how do I get back to reality?"

She quickly continued the conversation, "First, you will answer some questions and do so without lying. Can you do that?"

He hesitated until there was a loud splash very close to him. "Yes, of course, I can!"

Cilla directed, "You do understand I can tell when you are lying, and I do believe you just lied. Let's try this again. Will you tell the truth to my every question?"

The splashing was getting closer and closer. The lawyer looked with fear in every direction. Anticipating the next splash, he swallowed deeply and finally said, "Yes, I can and will tell the truth!"

Priscilla quickly asked, "Do you love my Aunt Dora?"

He yelled out, "The only person I love is myself! Your aunt is beautiful, and I would treat her like I would a prized possession!"

Cilla knowingly bursts out, "Now you are telling the truth!"

Priscilla calmly stated, "I can leave you here, or I can help you get back to reality. But what I want is for you to tell my family the whole truth. Do you agree with my terms?"

Smithfield chilled and tremblingly nods his head and spits out, "I agree to your terms. Now, get me out of here!"

Cilla directed the following, "I will return you to the rotting hickory stump. There my friends will see that you regain your normal size. You will go back inside and tell Dora and her father the truth and apologize for your lies. If they ask where I am, tell them I decided to go to bed and they can find me in my room. However, I will be listening to every word you say because I will be in the room with all of you."

Priscilla gave a hand signal, and Malcom leaped from his perch in the tree near the pond and grabbed both and dropped them near ground at the hickory stump.

There Cilla leaped on Sir Boss's back, and he raced to the back door of the house. He had chewed a hole in the screen door, and Priscilla leaped through the opening and hitched a ride on a mouse that was waiting for her.

She found Dora and her grandfather still seated in the dining room. Within a few minutes, Smithfield, still wet and shivering, came into the room.

When she saw her wet and slimy fiancé, Dora immediately jumped from her chair and exclaimed, "What happened, and where is Priscilla? Is she alright?"

Smithfield responded as directed, "She is fine. She went to her room to go to bed. You can check on her in a few minutes."

"I had somehow fallen into the pond, and Priscilla returned to the house. However, I have been doing some thinking and must tell you both something important." Looking directly at Professor Smyth, the defeated lawyer confessed, "Forgive me for being blunt, but I have decided to withdraw my proposal to marry Dora. She is way too valuable and beautiful; she has no business being tied down to an old bachelor like me.

In addition, I discovered I am not capable of loving her more than I love myself. I wanted to marry her to gain control of her potential inheritance and was more motivated after I discovered Priscilla's wealth. I am set in my ways and unable to change. Your daughter should find someone nearer her age, someone who would be dedicated to her happiness. I am confident I am not that person and will not change my mind. I apologize for harming or upsetting either of you in any way. I will now take my leave."

"By the way, I will send you a money draft to cover the expense you have incurred in the preparation of the wedding. If it is not adequate, please send me an estimate of the shortfall. Forgive me, I must go and get out of these wet clothes before I catch pneumonia." He then abruptly turned and left the house. Sneezing uncontrollably several times, Smithfield Goodfellow left the Smyth's home from which he would never return.

Priscilla saw the shock on Dora's face. She looked surprised and confused about the sudden change of plans. However, she shed only one tear and was not overwhelmed with grief. In fact, Cilla felt Dora seemed relieved that the marriage was called off.

Cilla raced up the stairs on the mouse's back to her bedroom where she found Sid waiting to return her to full size.

She quickly removed her wet garments, dried herself off, and jumped into her night clothes; within moments, she was ready for bed.

Dora and Cilla's grandfather soon after came into her bedroom to check on her. Dora was not upset but was simply concerned for Priscilla's safety and well-being.

The young orphan knew she had some serious prayers to say. She needed to thank God for Dora's, her grandfather's, and her own deliverance. Her yard friends had been the angels God used to deliver her new family from evil. Smithfield's plan to control the Smyth family's wealth was destroyed, and now Dora was free to find a more loving and compatible spouse. Priscilla smiled and fell into a well-deserved and peaceful sleep; she was exhausted. She had colorful dreams about her friends and many new adventures.

The End.

About the Authors

The author George B is an avid photographer and graphic designer. He retired as a senior scientist and shares his writing passion with his wife of forty-four years.

Linda B, the coauthor, is a teacher, registered nurse, and an accomplished musician. She teaches piano and plays for churches.

Our creative efforts are found in one previous children's book, *Priscilla's Prayer*, and now, in this children's book *Priscilla's Angels*. We have published two previous books written for older audiences: *Struggle and Survival a Boneyard Saga, Short Story Anthology* and *Volume 1, Mona Lisa on the Moon, Thirty-Two Thousand Years in the Making*.

www.ingramcontent.com/pod-product-compliance
Lightning Source LLC
Chambersburg PA
CBHW040154110726
48005CB00018B/2763